Loving Hard

*A Sojourn into
One Woman's
Heart*

T. K. Flowers

Copyright

Loving Hard Copyright © 2019 by T.K. Flowers

All rights reserved, including the right to reproduce this book in any form whatsoever without permission in writing from Argon Press, except for brief passages in connection with critical articles or reviews.

Published in the United States of America

by Argon Press

ISBN: 978-1-944815-90-5

(v 1.02)

www.ArgonPress.com

Table of Contents

Dedication 1

"I Fell into Your Eyes" 3
"Games We Play" 5
"Roller Coaster Ride" 7
"Shadows" 9
"Emotion" 11
"Camelot" 13
"Resurrection" 15
"Pushy Women" 17
"Dirty Laundry" 19
"Trust" 21
"Kiss Me" 23
"Dreams" 25
"Trembling" 27
"Knowing Love" 31
"Leave Me Waiting" 33
"Little Boy" 35
"Differences" 37
"Dedicated to Martha" 39
"Come In" 41
"I Have to Go Now" 43
"No, Don't Touch Me" 45

"The Closest Thing to Love" 47

"Driver" 49

"Man Enough" 51

"My Hero" 53

"I Trusted You" 55

"Passion Junkie" 59

"His Story" 61

"The Perfect Couple" 63

"The Visit" 65

"The Great Katharine" 67

"Making Love" 69

"The End" 71

Afterword 73

About the Author 75

About the Photographers 77

Dedication

My undying thanks to Steve, Marge, Larry and Peggy LeBel for giving me the courage to bear my soul in print. These words would still be a pile of papers on my desk without your encouragement.

Thank you to my editors for correcting every comma and period. Cousin Rose Marie Maclean, mentor Lou MacGready and friend Angie Guillen, you were the first to say, "I felt that, you're right."

Blessings and thanks to my sisterhood of girlfriends, so many, who held me together more times than petals in a field of roses these past years.

Never last, my thanks to "The Boss" who taught me how to love hard. You took me up to where mountains sing, down to the depths of myself and back again. My soul aches without you. Tell God I said, "Hi."

"The Eye Has It"

"I Fell into Your Eyes"

As I sat casually, sipping my drink, imagine my surprise when I looked up and promptly fell into your eyes.

Down, down I went to my demise; deep into the portals of your soul as I leapt into your eyes.

Farther from reality, through enchanted lands and dreams, down to where it seems only the innocent survive: when I fell into your eyes.

Down to where my heart etched on yours the wonder of this pure rapture, this loveliness amassed as I danced into your eyes.

How many minutes swept by us as our gazes lasted and if I had fasted, I could not feel such hunger, such passion of this size.

But the best part of the glory, as I fell forever backward, as I tripped on life and lasted in the wonder of your eyes was when I realized……

You fell into my eyes.

"The Games We Play"

"Games We Play"

You sneak into the room as I lay pretending to slumber, creeping up beside me so that I might not wake. I felt your presence before you entered the room. Shall I tell you of your aura meeting mine at the door?

    No, I think not……

I'll lay in watch as you attempt to rouse me. It's hard not to stir as your lips barely caress my brow. I turn ever so slightly, imitating sleep, waiting for the next advance in our covert game.

    What now, my awakener? Your move……

Oh, God, your touch-how unfair the chance you take. Come to me, make love to me, I concede the victory.

"Rollercoaster Ride"

"Roller Coaster Ride"

Loving you reminds me of the mountains. Sometimes you take me up so high, the air is clear: Smell the wind, crisp, clean and the joy fills me, cools me, nestles me gently in the wings of noble eagles.

And then you let me drop down to the valley of despair: crushed by the pressure of your lack of notice, swallowed by the darkness of your unconcern. The absence of your presence stifles the air.

Why do you take me up? Only to let me down? Is this the joy I give you? Is this roller coaster life to punish me, Or some past woman, I'll never know?

The constant up and downs of your love rob me, break me, heave me and yet I have no choice. I live only for you to send me high into the mountains. I willingly pay the price of the valleys.

"Shadows"

"Shadows"

Even as I sleep I can feel the massiveness of your frame spooned next to me: the muscle of your calf laying protectively over my legs, curling your body so close to mine. The separation between us is so minuet our auras mingle. I can feel your body hair softly tickle my spine As your chest heaves in and out, in slow, steady deliberation.

Softly, I feel steady kisses of breath gently caressing my neck. Your arms circle my body with strength to protect me; fearing I might curl away in the night your hand fondly cups my breast…so this is heaven.

Suddenly I awake, startled to find you're gone from my side, The bed cold and barren next to me… Please, God, say he was here, that it wasn't an apparition… Slowly the foggy cobwebs of sleep leave my brain….

No, you were never here at all…

"Flying High"

"Emotion"

Don't give me subtleties — Give me emotion!!!!!!!!
> Make me laugh.
> Make me cry.

The exhaustion from both is exhilarating. I love the fatigue each leaves me with. Bring me up-take me down-
> Don't let me just live: let me love life,
> Drink it in, smother in its wonder,
> Revel in its glory, gasp for breath from its terror.

Oh, God, give me emotion or let me die.

"Castles"

"Camelot"

Night is deep & still, making the world a stage of happy endings.

There sits Guinevere, stuck in a body her king finds comfort in no more. Lonely and desolate, she searches for her white knight to purge away the isolation she feels.

Where is her Lancelot on stead of white, red flag atop, waving in the breeze- to take her, if only for a little while, away, just away. To a garden of roses and lavender, the sweet smell permeating a cool wind.

He will carry her off to a haven of comfort and security. She knows he'll come.

Ah, its day now, and light has sharpened all the figures changing the outcome of the play.

Guinevere's silken gown has become blue jeans, the garden, a disheveled, old and musty house. Her king comes home with the stench of liquor on his breath, drunk and distant.

Lancelot's stallion is no more. Instead a police car speeds through town. Never stopping or caring for her dilemma.

Must the day always come and spoil the dreams a maiden has?

Oh, where is the night play with its softness and wonder?

>   Where is her Lancelot?
>   Where is her Camelot?
>   Where is away?
>   Pull the curtain down.

"Stairway to Heaven"

"Resurrection"

When my eyes weary at days end, I take solace in the memory of rapture in your arms.

When I tire of this day's earthly strife, I know the soft breath of your kiss would melt away the listlessness and bring new depth to my aching soul.

Why do only you and God have the power of resurrection?

I take comfort in knowing you can make me strong again.

"Pushy Women"

"Pushy Women"

"The perfect woman knows when to push and when not to," he said.

"I'm not her," she said. "I need to feel you deep within me now. You brought this want out in me, you opened up my vulnerability to your charm."

"Not now," he said, "Not now."

"How glad I am not to be your perfect women," she said. "To know the thrill of your touch and want more now, now as we speak, not when it's convenient. Not when I happen to be there at the bar's close, but now, now!"

"I'm really tired." he said. "Not now."

"You brought me out and opened up my passion!" she said. "And now, now that I need you, I can't push! I have to wait for you to make the choice? It's not fair to me. Now, please now, I need you now!" she said.

"The perfect woman doesn't push" he said. "Not now."

"So leave to find your perfect woman!" she said. "But for now, just now, one more time, bring me close to heaven. Let me die the little deaths that bring two people into one, now, now, please and I won't push again." she said.

"Now?" he said, "Push now."

"Layers and Piles"

"Dirty Laundry"

I try to work, go over my charts, but you're there — on my mind — like a blank page, waiting for inscription. I can't pigeon hole my thoughts. I can't file you away and go on to a new project — there, one more done and I can move on. Oh, no! There is no end to you. No precise starting or stopping point. Just there, in the way, eliminating the process of clear thought before it can even begin. And for what? There are no answers. I'm not sure there are even questions. Just this big internal, blank empty void of space filled with this entity, this craving. Why can't you be more like dishes? Once sorted, you wash them, dry them, and lock them up behind closed doors not to be bothered with until the need arises to use them again. No, you're more like dirty laundry. Even as you finish the last load, folded and placed securely away in a drawer, you look down and the clothes on your very back need washing.

There's never an end to laundry... There's never an end to you.

"Trust"

"Trust"

For some strange reason, I trust you.

You would rather not tell me,
    than to lie.

You won't hurt me,
    at least not on purpose.

You don't want to buy me,
    just rent me awhile.

You don't want to share my whole life,
    just a few precious moments of it.

How can so little of you be so much more than most?

Your distance is as much an aphrodisiac as it is a sorrow.

Still I trust you.

"Kisses"

"Kiss Me"

Just kiss me! I can't stand this waiting. The anticipation of your lips on mine is more than I can bear.

This want of your essence held tightly to mine, sends quivers to the center of my very being.

> Just kiss me!

Seeing you makes the minutes die until I can know the fullness of your mouth on mine.

The feel of your arm holding me so close I will have to peel away — your body excites me so.

> Just kiss me!

My body aches in expectation, I can wait no longer. I need to soak in the breath of life from those dear lips and feel the nectar of your soul creeping into mine, merging, blending, sending me to new heights of ecstasy.

I have to know, I have to know…

> Just kiss me!

"Dreaming"

"Dreams"

Was it just a dream?
Was he here at all?
Did he touch me so?
Did he kiss me long?
Did I want it 'till it seemed to be?
Will he come again?
Does he think of me?

Am I dreaming still,
as I feel his hand?
Did it come to this?
Do I need this man?
Do I want him so?
Does he want me too?
Will he call again?
Will I last till then?

"Trembling"

"Trembling"

He's here, loving and kind, then not a word for weeks.

And yet the first moment my eyes touch sight with his,
> I tremble…

Why? I don't know. He's distant and then gone. He never said I was special.

It's just the look of gentleness, the touch of sincerity, the kiss of passion. This he gives to me,
> and then I tremble…

I spent so long not letting a man get to me. Caring but now close, loving yet not letting go. Then him.

His mere touch makes me sigh,
> and then I tremble.

Distance from him, I thought was the answer. I tried "out of sight out of mind." But no, it didn't work. I'm so scared he will just trash me, blow me off unconcerned.

I know he will, he has before. I don't need this, I have things to do. Do I sound confused? I am.

He doesn't even want me,
> And then I tremble….

How can I let this man humiliate me so? I ask for him to come to me. He said he would and then I'm left to wait, two, three, four times.

I have my pride. I can't ask again. Now I have to wait for him,
> And all the while I tremble.

"Seeds for Life"

"Pure Joy"

"Knowing Love"

How do I know I love you?

In the middle of the day, I hear a word that triggers a memory of time we've spent together. Or I smell the air and a bit of your essence meanders in from a distant place.

Suddenly a light comes into my eyes, I give a kind of half smile and a heart filled sigh.

>That's how I know I love you.

"Waiting"

"Leave Me Waiting"

I would give my heart to be a book, leathery ice-cold cover weighing heavily in your hands. I would savor the feel of your fingers flipping saucily through my pages. I would venerate the caress of your warm glance studying my passages.

It would bring me such pleasure.

I would give my soul to be a report you thoroughly examine over and over and over until every word was precise. Then I would know what it was like to be cherished by you.

The best I can do is to leave you to your work, the only life force you seem to need, and leave me waiting.

"Youth and Innocence"

"Little Boy"

How long has it been?

Too many days to count since
I've seen the glow of your smile.
I watch the window hoping for
the reflection of that boyish
charmed image peeking back at me.

Do I bring the boy out in you
as much as you bring the woman
out in me?

"Black and White"

"Differences"

You're black, non-reflective, so accurate, so precise.
I'm red, so changing, a mirror image of what surrounds me.
Why do I love you?
Why are we friends when so much separates us?
Differences abound…

It's easy!
I need you to make me more together.
You need me to bring you out.
Let' do lunch!

"The Royal Couple"

"Dedicated to Martha"

What you do is who you are.

I take your badge and gun to the very center of my heart, as I do you, for they are one and the same, divided not.

I choose to share you with the people you serve, instead of not having you at all.

The best I can do is comfort the tensions of the night from your body when you finally come home to me at dawn.

And when I send you out again, no matter what the last words on my lips, you'll know in your inner soul,

I love you.

Every day is ours... Every night I wait... Every moment I pray...

In memory of Officer Terry Thompson, Burton Police Department, shot and killed while responding to a burglary alarm July 5, 1983.

"Come In"

"Come In"

I wish you could crawl deep within my body so you could feel this need I have for you.

I wish you could see through my eyes your handsomeness and charm.

From within my heart you could feel your tenderness.

From within my senses you could savor your smell so sweet, your taste so pungent.

Come in now and see the you only the deep in me can ever know.

Come in, now.

Come in.

"The Journey"

"I Have to Go Now"

I left you sitting there for fear you would touch me:
Fear I couldn't respond;
Fear I wouldn't make the right move;
Fear I couldn't show how long I have waited
      for that very moment,
         that very touch.
I left you sitting there for fear…
      You wouldn't touch me at all…

"Layers"

"No, Don't Touch Me"

No, don't touch me!
Let me just lie in your bed a sweet while longer.

No, don't touch me!
Just let me feel your warmth, let me take in the lingering wonder of your body in the silken sheets.

No, don't touch me!
Leave me to gaze lovingly on the spot where your head nestled in the pillow last night.

Let me take comfort in the aroma of your essence in this haven from harm.

Ah yes, awaken all my senses,

    part by part,

    layer by layer,

    piece by piece…

Now, come to me, touch me,

    make me whole.

"The Rose"

"The Closest Thing to Love"

I give to you the closest thing I know to the pureness of my heart.

It has the softness of an angel's kiss, each section a velvet impersonator.

Its essence fondly permeates the room.

Its hue imitates regal blood, as you are my liege.

The wonder of this gift of pleasure-pain, its gentleness cloaked in thorns of protection, is all I know that can reveal the simple, gentle love I have for you…

I give to you a rose.

"The Road to Life"

"Driver"

I sit silently watching the cars parade by: each with a secret desire hidden behind the wheel.

Every mile covered heightens the anticipation, every turn, the craving magnifies.

How many miles must be driven before the climax is implosive, tearing the guts from the man, separating the soul from the woman?

Desire driving on and on and on…

      God help us.

"Strong and Yet"

"Man Enough"

You were man enough to wake feelings deep within me I had buried years ago.

No one would touch my heart again!

No one would touch my private passion!

This I would give to no mortal man.

You were man enough to wake feelings I had put to rest many painful nightmares ago.

And you were man enough to put those feelings aside, with no disgust in the knowledge I had been savagely taken and tossed askew.

You showed no regret for the first touch you gave me, never wanting to pull back, repulsed, and then to go away, as I had felt from other men not of your gallantry.

You were man enough to say we could take care of it together, we would work it out.

I owe you my new-found passion.

I owe you my joy when only you, out of the masses, were man enough to be my friend.

I owe to you the need I have to feel you deep inside now, a long-lost fever I had never hoped to feel again.

"Together Forever"

"My Hero"

I'll never have you in perspective to humanity, you know.

You'll always be larger than life to me.

My Don Quixote dreamer, my John Wayne hero.

Can you ever be just a regular man, a standard man?

No, I think not. In my story book of life, You will always be Lancelot, my hero of the night, standing grandly next to mortal men, I pity them their normalcy.

It must be a tough job, being an idol to the masses.

Please I beg of you, don't fall from this pedestal I have contrived.

My heart would die if I knew you bleed as mere average men do.

Let's stay in the mystical forever… You and I.

Through eternity I will be your Guinevere,

You will always be my liege.

"Empty"

"I Trusted You"

I tried to play it safe knowing the havoc you could bring to me.
    I watched you until I was sure you cared.
    Until I was sure you wouldn't hurt me.
    Until I thought you wanted me.
And then I let go to you…

I let go as a powerful wave surged through my body.
I trusted you.
I let you touch me places I held from other men for years.
    It happened so quickly, beside you talking.
    Then, naked to you; both body and soul.
    Your lips hovering on my neck.
I feel it still.

I hate you for waking in me feelings I had laid to rest years ago.
And then, just then, when you knew I was most vulnerable, you touched my heart.
How dare you?
I trusted you, and what did you do?
You walked right up and touched my heart.

Grabbed it from my chest with your clenched hand, pulled it out before me, beating, pulsing.
Then you ripped it from my body, squeezing out the life force, a jumbled mass dripping onto the floor.

Yet I lived, and so I will.

      Nothing but a walking empty cavity.

I trusted you.

"Soaring"

"Narrow Vision"

"Passion Junkie"

You have made me a passion junkie, stealing each kiss I can from those dear lips while living in dread of how long I must wait before I might get my fix again.

I lie here, in the small hours of the night trying to remember every word uttered, every subtle wanting touch I stole from you as I begged, in God's mercy, for you not to go.

Leaving this bed means embracing the fear that memory of your arms engulfing me might fade from my power of recollection bringing on new craving for your touch.

I cling to every moment in your repose.

Of all the worldly opiates to tempt the soul, why have you become my drug of choice, my angel of addiction?

"Pride"

"His Story"

I come to our bed at shift change, early in the dawn, pulling from you, the woman I've chosen to share my life, strength which I can't bear to tell you I need.

I can't spill my guts about the child I found in pieces in the street.
I can't load you with the burden of the man I shot tonight.
These I must carry.

You took me for better or worse, not for the badge.
You raise the children, I'll face the odds.
My recklessness, my cynical nature, help to make me whole…
But whole as to what?

Though I can't ask, listen with your heart.
Let me tell you of the child, let me tell you of the man, not to frighten you or make you wonder of the life you've chosen, but to know I need to talk when words cannot say how crazy my life can be.

Keep me from the drink whose poison kills.
Stop me from the paths of destruction others have taken.
This is the life I've chosen.
Love me and let me live it.
Just don't let me know you share the burden too.

"Secure as the Moon"

"The Perfect Couple"

The perfect man knows how to see past a women's façade into her soul: knowing when she needs to be held, just for a little while 'till she can regroup and come out strong again.

The perfect man knows too that when his life is not quite right, the perfect woman will hold him. No one will know of the small time of insecurities the perfect man can sometimes feel.

Now we have the perfect couple, both only human, wanting to please themselves, and yet each other and to know together they are strong.

One and/or the other or both, but together always and in each other's arms, secure.

"The Weeds of Life"

"The Visit"

I went to see your mom today.

She says she prays for you constantly.

I told her the kids were fine.

She knew, she had been keeping track.

We talked awhile about how much I love you, that you were my entire world.

"He always acts so tough," I said, "but his heart is the gentlest I've ever known."

"He's very special to me too. He always was my favorite," she said.

I told her I'd be back to talk.

She said she'd be right there waiting.

Next time I go, I need to take the clippers, dear.

      The grass is so high I could hardly see her stone.

"Resolute"

"The Great Katharine"

Dear, Dear Katharine, how do I commence?

Forever the lover, more important,

the friend, to the indomitable Spence.

How hard it must have been for you

on the day he died, to have to walk away

and to never see him hence.

The mistress always loves them most

and yet has the least to say

when men are called to our sweet God

and their wives come into play.

I've heard you were barred the funeral stop

or decorum kept you away.

The cemetery was your last goodbye

early the next day.

I know he's in your heart right now.

He'll always be there hence.

Because God so loved the world

He went and gave us Spence.

Dedicated to the great love affair between Katharine Hepburn and Spencer Tracy.

"The Nature of Life"

"Making Love"

Making love isn't a single act, a hot hour or even a long torrid afternoon. It should be a lifestyle of caring.

Making love is a collection of events, an all day, every day, life time commitment to sharing. Love is a verb, a string of one action step after another. Love is small touches, ear nibbles, kisses on the neck from dawn to dusk, building, growing and developing till they cumulate into a giant release.

Making love isn't just saying, "I love you," but more like, "When you're not here, I'm empty." It's not "How do you feel?" but more of "You're sick. Go home, take a nap."

Making love is "Lock the door after I go and take a bath, you'll sleep better."

Making love is a collection of random acts of kindness. It can be a small white lie that betters someone's day without harm.

Making love is a way of life.

Don't just say you love me, show me.

Please, I beg you, make love to me.

"Alone"

"The End"

"He's gone," he said in a whisper, "I didn't want you to hear somewhere else."

"You're brave," I said crying blindly, "to call and tell me. What now?"

"The funeral," he said more crisply, "he didn't want to be buried in his blues."

"I can't breathe," I said.

"You must," he said.

"My family, my future all gone," I said desperately. "He took them with him."

"His last wish was that you know he loved you," he said with pity.

"I always knew, all through the years," I said.

"He loved the moon," I said, "and watching it through the trees."

"Huh?" he said, the concept being lost on him.

Men don't talk to buddies about relishing the moon.

Only those that love them as deep as infinity know.

"He's really gone?" I said.

"Yes," he said.

Then they both were, and I was truly and eternally alone.

"Resurrection"

Afterword

I thought existence as I knew it was over, for surely, I could not live with part of my soul gone forever. Life would never be the same again.

God in his wisdom sent me someone to carry me through the next part of my life, a calming, protective soul to compliment mine.

Life is a journey. Often, in youth, like a carnival ride but hopefully in the mature years, the experience is more like a gentle ride down a calming country stream.

Thank you, Kenny, for bringing me to quiet water.

About the Author

T.K. Flowers is a 5th generation resident of Genesee County, Michigan with roots in family horticulture of over 170 years. She describes herself as a nerd that "sometimes lets the right brain fly!" This is one woman's story of a love affair.

T.K. says, "If you have loved hard, you will understand. If not, maybe this will give you the intrigue and courage to try."

T.K. Flowers prays you will have the chance to love hard and hopes, for your sanity, you never will.

Ms. Flowers writes about personal experiences in her life while sitting on her veranda. She hopes that in sharing, she finds others who have experienced love as deeply as she has

T.K. invites you to dive in and enjoy.

About the Photographers

Black and white photos are by Gary Pearce, a freelance photographer. Gary finds detail and drama in the cinema we call natural habitat.

All prints are used with explicit permission from Mr. Pearce's private collection gathered as he has "wondered the earth".

T.K. Flowers is greatly indebted to Mr. Pearce for his collection as his imagery punctuates each poem.

~

Back cover photo is by professional award-winning photographer Penny Messer. **Penny's from Heaven,** Photography and Fine Art.

Penny is a long-standing resident and community enthusiast from Swartz Creek, Michigan. T.K. thanks her for her excellent portrait and friendship.

www.ingramcontent.com/pod-product-compliance
Lightning Source LLC
Chambersburg PA
CBHW030004050426
42451CB00006B/113